WINNING AT WORK READINESS

STEP-BY-STEP GUIDE TO

EFFECTIVE JOB HUNTING & CAREER PREPAREDNESS

Susan Henneberg

ROSEN
PUBLISHING®

New York

Published in 2015 by The Rosen Publishing Group, Inc.
29 East 21st Street, New York, NY 10010

Library of Congress Cataloging-in-Publication Data

Henneberg, Susan.
Step-by-step guide to effective job hunting & career preparedness/Susan Henneberg.—First Edition.
        pages cm.—(Winning at work readiness)
Audience: Grades 7–12.
Includes bibliographical references and index.
ISBN 978-1-4777-7774-9 (library bound)—ISBN 978-1-4777-7812-8 (pbk.)—
ISBN 978-1-4777-7777-0 (6-pack)
1. Job hunting—Juvenile literature. 2. Résumés (Employment)—Juvenile literature. 3. Employment interviewing—Juvenile literature. I. Title.
HF5382.7.H464 2015
650.14—dc23

2014006325

Manufactured in the United States of America

CONTENTS

INTRODUCTION

Welcome to the twenty-first-century job search! Have you decided it is time to join the adult world and get a paying job? If you have, congratulations. Holding a job can provide many benefits. The money you earn can pay for gas, car insurance, cell phone bills, and future college tuition. You can gain valuable employment skills. You can connect your schoolwork to real-life situations. You will build confidence and maturity. In addition, you can explore different career interests. Working can help you prepare for a successful future.

For many teens, however, getting a job is difficult. You probably don't have a lot of experience. Your work skills may be minimal. You may not have reliable transportation. You may have to work around school and family commitments. Nevertheless, you do not have to let these issues become barriers to employment. Look around your community. You will find thousands of teens like you working and enjoying productive jobs. They are working in the fast-food, retail, and child care industries. They operate the rides at amusement parks, teach children how to swim at public pools, and guide visitors at national parks.

These teens are learning and practicing some important skills. They take advantage of opportunities to show leadership. They understand the importance of collaboration with coworkers. They become top problem solvers by approaching potential issues with creativity and imagination. They approach conflicts with a win-win attitude. How do they do it? How do teens survive and thrive in the adult world? How can you join this world and start preparing for your future?

Teens play a valuable role in the adult world by working in businesses such as restaurants.

Most successful job seekers have used a step-by-step approach. What does this mean? How can a systematic method toward finding a job and preparing for a career help you? First, you will understand the importance of identifying your skills, abilities, and interests before looking for a job. Setting job search goals will efficiently guide you toward a job that fits you. Next, you will identify the resources you need. Like many teens, you are probably a pro at using social media. You will learn that your network of friends is your most important tool. You will discover other innovative techniques for finding a great job as well. The next steps involve job applications, résumés, and cover letters. You'll need to use your most polished written communication skills. If you have done the beginning steps well, you will be invited to interviews. Your successful oral communication skills here may net you a job. You'll have to shine. Finally, you'll need to think ahead to your future beyond your first job. How will you be able to use your job search experiences to explore different careers?

If all these steps to getting a job sound daunting, don't worry. Breaking a difficult process down into separate steps makes it manageable. This step-by-step approach doesn't just work for finding a job. You can use it to achieve any goal that lies ahead. Whenever you feel overwhelmed, you can reflect back on the problem-solving skills you learned in the process of finding a job. Examining your assets, setting goals, identifying resources, promoting your best self, and parlaying your experiences toward new goals are steps that you can use your whole life. Good luck!

Chapter 1

WHO AM I? ASSESSING SKILLS, ABILITIES, AND INTERESTS

A re you excited about looking for a job? Are you ready to just jump into the job hunt and start filling out applications everywhere? You might want to slow down. You may be ready to work, but you may not want to work just anywhere. Talk to the adults around you. Ask them about how much they enjoy their jobs. Some may say they love them—they can't wait to get to work each day. Others might have a different response. They may say they don't like their jobs. It may be hard to get motivated to go to work each day. Which way would you like to feel about your job? What makes the difference? How can you get a job that gets you excited each day?

ANSWERING THE QUESTION: WHO AM I?

It may not be realistic to think that you can get your dream job right away. But you can start putting yourself on the right path. The first step of that path is important. You need to know who you are. The more you know about yourself, the closer you can come to a job that makes you happy. Time spent figuring out your talents,

Your school counselor can be a great resource for job search tips and strategies.

skills, interests, and abilities will pay off. You will not find yourself in a job each day where you struggle to stay focused. You will not be bored. Instead, you will be challenged to do your best. You will be motivated to succeed.

There are many tools you can use to help you with this task of figuring out who you are. Some of them are as easy as daydreaming. Some tools you can find at school. Your school counselor or career center assistant can provide a great deal of help. Your school or public library will have books that can guide you through this process. The Internet, too, has some good online tools for self-discovery.

WHAT DO I LOVE TO DO?

Wouldn't it be great to have a job that paid you to do what you already love to do? The first step to finding that job is to identify your interests. Make a list of how you spend your time. What seems to capture your attention the most? What is your favorite subject in school? What extracurricular activities do you do? Some teens might put sports on their list. Certainly many teens would put video games. Maybe you like to sing or play an instrument. Or maybe you spend a lot of time with your pets. All of these pursuits are clues that could lead to a great job.

Use a notebook to list these activities. Or you could use your computer, smartphone, or tablet. Popplet, bubbl.us, and mySimpleSurface are good online brainstorming tools. Brainstorming is a way to just think freely without stopping or analyzing your choices. One idea will lead to the next, until you have pages of clues to where you might want to work.

WHAT AM I GOOD AT?

The next step is to list your best skills. Start listing the things that you do well. Or maybe your friends or family have complimented you on something you do. Why is this step important? You are more likely to be happy at a job where you can be successful. You will stick with it without getting bored or discouraged.

A skill is a developed aptitude or ability. For example, you may love to play basketball and have excelled in the sport. What are the skills here? You may have good hand-eye coordination. You may also have good physical agility and balance. You can make decisions quickly when calling a play. You work well on a team without having to be the star. All these skills can transfer to a job. Most workplaces want employees who work well with others and can think on their feet. Furthermore, physical skills

9

Taking the time to list your skills and abilities will pay off with a job that is a good fit for you.

can be important if you work with kids in an after-school program or camp.

CATEGORIZING YOUR SKILLS

There are many ways to categorize your skills. One way is to organize them into these three areas: skills with things, skills with information, and skills with people. Most people have abilities in all three areas. But most find that they have more skills in one category than the other two. The first grouping is skills with things. Do you have skills that involve moving quickly and easily with your body, such as playing sports or the guitar? Do you have

DEVELOPING YOUR SOFT SKILLS

Many people who do the hiring for their businesses differentiate between hard and soft skills. You can see hard skills. Hard skills are abilities such as playing an instrument, changing a tire, or calculating profit and loss. These abilities are important. However, hiring professionals say that even more essential are the soft skills an employee brings to the job. Soft skills are qualities such as dependability, honesty, and motivation. Employers want workers who show up on time, are enthusiastic, and are able to work with a team. A boss can teach a worker to operate a cash register competently. But he or she needs more than that from an employee. The boss needs the employee to arrive with a great attitude, communicate courteously to customers, and act maturely at all times.

skills using objects and materials? For example, do you make jewelry or cook great dinners? Can you put together a computer? Have you trained your dog to do tricks? Take some time to jot down the answers to questions like these.

The second category is skills with information and ideas. At school, are you a good researcher or investigative reporter? Do your peers tell you that you always have good ideas about what to write? Do they rely on you to plan group projects or figure out the math homework? Can you easily find the data you need to support your essays? People who have skills in this area come up with great plots for stories. They are good at problem solving. They are also good at keeping track of details. They would be helpful partners in a biology lab in school.

People who have good skills when it comes to information and ideas can become valued problem solvers in the workplace.

The third grouping is skills with people. Here are some questions to ask yourself to see if communicating or working effectively with people is a strength for you. Do your friends ask you to listen to their

problems? Can you give clear instructions in telling someone how to do something? Do teachers rely on you to keep a discussion going? Are you a leader who can persuade a group to follow your suggestions? Do you enjoy tutoring and coaching? All these are signs of good people skills.

Hopefully by now you have long lists of skills and abilities. Now it's time to narrow them down. Choose the top ten skills. These are the ones at which you are the best and enjoy the most. In what category are they? Are they from mainly one or spread across two or three? These skills are major clues to the job you want.

If your skills are in the first category, you may want to think about applying to be an umpire, prep cook, or landscaper. If the second category had many entries, you could think about medical billing, research assistant, and legal aide. Teens who listed skills in the third category could apply at retail stores, amusement parks, and day care centers.

It may seem time-consuming to make these lists. However, time spent identifying your skills will pay off. Examining your abilities carefully beforehand may help you avoid getting a job that you will not like. Instead, you can concentrate your job hunting on positions that you are good at, like, and can give you a head start into your future. The ancient Greek saying "know thyself" is a great first step to getting a job you will love.

Chapter 2

BECOMING A JOB DETECTIVE AND CREATING A PLAN

You have taken the time to figure out your best skills. You know what category of job type would interest you the most. You have a general idea of what kind of job you want. What is the next step? Again, it is not jumping into the job hunt. To do that without a plan would be like heading across the country without a road map. You may get somewhere, but it will not likely be in the place you want. Taking the first job you are offered may work out. Or you may wish you had looked harder for a job that better fit your skills and interests. A step-by-step plan will help you find the right job for your skills.

There are three basic steps to creating a job search plan. First, you need to target the places that fit your skills. Next, you need to identify the people who can help with employment opportunities. Finally, you need a way of tracking your progress toward your job search. If these steps sound complicated, they do not have to be. You have everything you need. You have a list of your top skills and interests. You have a network of family, friends, acquaintances, and the friends of all these people. You probably have a notebook or binder that you can use to keep track of your job search. Teens who like computers can use word processing or spreadsheet programs such as Microsoft Word or Excel. Are you ready to start?

FINDING THE RIGHT WORKPLACES FOR YOU

Whether you live in a large city or a small town, there are places to work that fit your interests and skills. Start by making a list of all the places you can think of where you can use your skills. For example, if you are good with animals, you might list the local animal shelter, pet stores, and grooming shops. If you are clever with information and ideas, libraries and bookstores might make

Targeting places that match your top interests and skills can result in a job that is fun and rewarding.

your list. Those who like to work with people might include any place that has a lot of customer contact. Amusement parks, mall stores, and day care centers might be fun places to try, too.

Next, you will need to prioritize your list. Decide what your top choices are and put them first. You will need to take into consideration the pay and location of each place. Work sites that are far from where you live will take money for gas, parking, or public transportation. Workplaces close to home or near public transportation can save time and money.

NETWORKING YOUR WAY INTO A JOB

Just about every expert in job searching stresses the importance of networking. He or she knows that most jobs are never advertised. You need to find out about these positions from the people who work at the companies. First, create a short "elevator" speech that tells everyone what kind of job you are looking for and why you are qualified for it. An elevator speech should take the amount of time to ride in an elevator from one floor to the next.

Then identify everyone who can help you find a job. The following is one method. Draw three concentric circles on notebook paper. In the center, put your first-degree contacts. First-degree contacts are the people who are closest to you, such as family members, good friends, neighbors, coaches, and church or scout leaders.

The next circle is your second-degree acquaintances. These are people you know, but you really don't have a close relationship with them. For instance, they could include the people you say "hi" to at the gym, neighbors down the street, teachers and counselors, and friends of friends to whom you have been introduced. The last level contains the people you want to meet. They are the ones who can get you that great job you want.

CREATING A PROFESSIONAL MESSAGE

How professional is your voice-mail message? Many teens think it is cool to begin it with a blast of their favorite music. They then follow it with a funny request to leave a message. A potential employer might not be so amused. If you want to be taken seriously, you will need to prepare a voice-mail message that clearly identifies you and politely asks the caller to leave a message.

If a hiring manager "Googled" you, what would he or she find? This type of search is an increasingly common practice. You would be smart to make sure your online presence is as professional as possible. Some suggestions for enhancing your digital footprint include the following: Ask friends to untag you from photos that are embarrassing. Change privacy settings on social networks so that only close friends can see your posts. Create a fun and productive image online. Improve your academic digital footprint. For example, enter online writing contests or start a blog devoted to your school interests, such as film, theater, physics, sports, or music. Upload positive photos, blogs, profiles, and reviews to social media. Your online reputation will likely follow you for the rest of your career.

Any person on your list can provide a lead to a job. Writer Sarah Mahoney suggests a phone conversation such as this: "My mom is in your book group, and she suggested I ask if you could use some help with your landscaping business." End your call in a way that leaves an opening for checking back. She suggests, for example: "Thanks for taking my call. Let me give you my number, so if things change or you hear of anything else, you can contact me. And is it OK if I check back with you in a week or so?" Be prepared if you need to leave a voice mail. Make sure you are clear and concise about what you are asking.

Your friends who have jobs can be a great resource. That's how Hot Dog on a Stick human resources manager Midori Cronky fills her open jobs. In a 2013 *Press Enterprise* story, she said, "Once you had a good crew, they would always refer other people that they would think would be a good fit." If you really want a job, you need to be fearless in telling everyone you know that you are job hunting.

Many job hunters use cold calling as a strategy. Cold calling means contacting someone you likely do not know to ask about job possibilities. You can write a letter or an e-mail, and include a résumé. This method may work well if your interests and experience closely match the needs of the particular workplace. Practice ahead of time a short speech that tells who you are and why you are contacting that workplace. You may have to leave a voice mail. Finish the call, letter, or e-mail with your complete contact information. Ask if you can periodically check back to see if anything has opened up. Employers may be impressed by your persistence. If they seem annoyed, though, discontinue the contacts.

Tech-savvy teens will want to use the Internet to find a job. There are dozens of job hunting websites, some specifically for teens. Because there are thousands of people reading and following up on the jobs, your chances of actually getting a job through such websites are slim. Your time is better spent actively looking for jobs that are not yet advertised. Matt Youngquist, president of Career Horizons, told National Public Radio in 2011, "At least 70 percent, if not 80 percent, of jobs are not published." He added, "The vast majority of hiring is friends and acquaintances hiring other trusted friends and acquaintances." This drawback doesn't mean you shouldn't check job websites. Still, your best bet for a potential job is your network.

Try rehearsing your "elevator speech" in front of a mirror until you can clearly and concisely tell potential employers who you are and why they should hire you.

STAYING ORGANIZED DURING THE JOB HUNT

A good way to organize your network is by using a spreadsheet. You can make one by drawing lines in a notebook. Computer

Researching company websites on the Internet to note human resources managers' names and addresses and using software applications to help you organize networking contacts will help you map out a path for your job hunt and monitor your progression.

applications such as Microsoft Excel and Google Spreadsheets enable you to create and manage spreadsheets easily. If you have a smartphone, there are handy apps for organizing contacts. You will want to record names, titles (such as human resources manager or supervisor), the names of businesses or organizations, phone numbers, e-mail addresses, and physical addresses. You will want

to leave space to record the dates for when you have contacted these people. Having each level of network alphabetized by last name will be helpful.

Career experts tell job hunters to treat looking for a job like it is a job. Although you may not want to spend an eight-hour day looking for work, you do need to be serious about it. Each day, set goals for yourself. Decide how many people you will contact or follow up with. For example, you may choose to call five people and e-mail five more. Then you may hop onto your bike, a bus, or a subway to visit five workplaces. After you have made initial contact, you'll need to follow up. A good time to wait before following up on a job is one week.

Reserve a column in your notebook or spreadsheet for follow-up contacts and their results. You'll need to note whether you spoke to someone in person or left a message. You may be adding new contacts continually as you receive new leads. Using these steps of identifying the right workplaces, creating a vast network of contacts, and then keeping your contacts organized will pay off. You will be able to track your progress toward obtaining the best job for you.

Chapter 3

PRESENTING YOUR BEST SELF: JOB APPLICATIONS, RÉSUMÉS, AND COVER LETTERS

So you have put together a considerable list of possible workplaces. Now you'll need to create the professional communications that can get you an interview. Many businesses and organizations require you to fill out applications. Taking the time to do these neatly and accurately is essential. Including a résumé and cover letter will let employers know that you take your job search seriously. These documents need to look professional. Many employers report that an impressive cover letter has made the difference in their callbacks. Follow these suggested steps to create polished applications, résumés, and cover letters.

MAKING YOUR JOB APPLICATIONS STAND OUT

In 2012, the U.S. Department of Labor reported that the top jobs by far for teens were in the leisure and hospitality sector. These jobs include positions at pools, camps, and restaurants. The second largest job group was in retail trade. Think of all the stores where you regularly shop. Would you like to work there, too? These

Application for Employment

Please fill out form completely for employment consideration. Print and fax or mail when completed.

Position Applied For:	
Social Security No.:	

Full legal		
	Last Name	First
Home		
Street		
	City	State

E-mail Address:

Education:

Highest school grade

Do you have a high school

Number of years of post high

Name and Location of Educational Institution:	Degree Received	

A neatly completed application tells employers that you value accuracy and attention to detail. Some businesses ask job seekers to submit online applications that are posted on their websites.

sectors are great places to begin asking for job applications. There are a wide variety of jobs in hospitality and retail for almost every type of personality.

In some workplaces, you can ask an employee for an application. He or she may hand you one to take home or fill out on the spot, or you may be directed to the manager. You may be asked to fill out an online application. Whether the application is filled out by hand or completed online, the best practices are the same. They need to be neat and accurate. If your handwriting is sloppy, this is a good time to learn how to write neatly. Messy writing will not impress an employer. For reference, have a résumé with you that contains your

RÉSUMÉ DOS AND DON'TS

Keep the following points in mind when you are compiling your résumé:

>) Do not list hobbies or interests unless they relate to the job.

>) Don't lie. Your employer will find out sooner or later that you included incorrect information. You may lose your job.

>) Choose type that is simple and classic, such as Times New Roman or Arial. Do not use fancy fonts.

>) Keep the résumé to one side of one page.

>) Include a separate page for three references that have agreed to recommend you. These references are three adults who know you well. Include each name, a title if there is one, and the contact information. You cannot use family members.

>) Use plain white or off-white paper.

total work history. Make sure every blank is filled in on the application, even if you write that the question doesn't apply to you. Otherwise, the employer will think you overlooked it.

John Challenger, CEO of career agency Challenger Gray & Christmas, gave the following advice in a 2012 Fox Business article. "Go to a store and ask to meet the manager," he advised teens. "Tell them you are reliable and get along with customers. Ask if they have any opportunities available. If they don't, keep coming back and checking. It's not too aggressive. But it's persistent." Cutter Matlock, the hiring manager of a Maryland Six Flags

America park, also talked about the important qualities that teen job seekers need to have. In a 2013 *Family Circle* magazine article, Matlock said, "We hire something like 2,500 seasonal employees for this park every year. About half are returnees. But the rest are new. As long as kids can follow through with the online application process, and convey that they are confident, passionate, and fun people, we're interested."

CREATING A RÉSUMÉ THAT DAZZLES

All teen job seekers should have a résumé. It is important even if your employment history is spotty or sparse. A résumé presents your work history. It also has all your contact information. It lists your skills such as CPR and first-aid training. Hiring managers use résumés to help them screen out the people they do not want to interview.

A 2012 study by the employment company, The Ladders, showed some interesting data about résumés. It found that hiring managers spend only six seconds looking at a résumé. They also look first at particular areas of a résumé. They are looking for specific information that will help them make a decision. What does that mean for you? Your résumé must have all the information an employer needs to determine whether you can do the job. In addition, the information has to appear where the employer expects to find it.

Start by brainstorming all your paid and unpaid jobs. Include babysitting or yard work. Include any work experience at school, such as answering phones, filing, or aiding a teacher. Add any volunteer work you have done or internships you have had, especially if the experiences are relevant to this job search. Do you regularly help out at Sunday school, operate the snack bar during

Claire Perez
423 Oak Street
Durham, TX 92921
(613) 925-4765
cperez@t-link.net

Work Experience

Landscaping Assistant   Perez Family, Durham, TX   *March 2014–Present*
- Cut lawn weekly
- Maintained lawn mowing equipment
- Trimmed and pruned bushes, hedges, and trees
- Planted and maintained flower and vegetable gardens

Office Aide   *Lincoln High School, Durham, TX   September 2013–December 2013*
- Answered phone and directed calls to appropriate staff members
- Sorted and delivered daily mail
- Filed letters and other documents
- Made photocopies for teachers
- Delivered messages to teachers and counselors

Child Care Provider   *Martin Family, Durham, TX   June 2013–September 2013*
- Provided a safe environment for three small children
- Prepared healthy meals and snacks
- Supervised homework and fun activities

Education

- 3.0 GPA
- Skilled in Microsoft Word, PowerPoint, and Excel
- Bilingual in Spanish and English

Certifications

Red Cross Babysitting Course, May 2013
CPR, Forest Hospital, June 2013

References available on request

A résumé lists clearly and concisely all of your work experience, with the most recent job first.

football season, or coach youth sports? All these activities include work experience.

For each job, list the skills you used. By describing what you have done, an employer will see what you are capable of doing. Your complete contact information should be located at the top of the résumé. Your contact information should include your name, address, telephone number, and e-mail address. Many teens have fun e-mail addresses such as "gutsygurl" or "studmuffin." This casual type of e-mail address shows that you aren't serious or that you are not professional. Use a free e-mail company, such as Gmail, Yahoo!, or Microsoft Outlook, to create an address that is appropriate. Having your first initial and last name in your e-mail address is considered professional.

List your jobs chronologically, with the most recent one first. Include the dates and duration of the jobs. Use action verbs to describe the exact duties, and write the details in phrases instead of complete sentences. Include any certifications you have earned, such as CPR or first responder. Most employment experts would agree that the physical appearance of a résumé is as important as the content. Keep your résumé looking clean and uncluttered. The Internet and libraries can provide models to look at while you are putting your résumé together.

HIGHLIGHT YOUR SKILLS WITH COVER LETTERS

Always include a cover letter with your résumé. This brief letter goes on top of, or covers, the résumé and introduces you to a potential employer. In this letter, you tell the employer that you are writing to apply for a certain job. You can highlight the qualifications, skills, and experience from your résumé that match the job for which you are applying. You can also explain why you want the

Claire Perez
423 Oak Street
Durham, TX 92921
(613) 925-4765
cperez@t-link.net

August 30, 2014

Mr. James Lucas
Manager
Green Leaf Nursery
224 Main Street
Durham, TX 92921

Dear Mr. Lucas:

An employee of yours, Jason Brown, informed me that there was a part-time position open in the sales yard at Green Leaf Nursery. Because of my interest and experience in the landscaping industry, I would like to apply for the position.

I have been taking care of plants, trees, and lawns for most of my life. Our home's extensive collection of twenty houseplants has been my responsibility since I was twelve. I have maintained our outdoor landscaping since then as well. All are green and healthy.

In the spring of 2014, at my neighbors' request, I began a neighborhood landscaping business. I currently cut and trim the lawns of six homes on a weekly basis. I fertilize, prune, and aerate as needed. In addition, I add seasonal color with annual plants. I have learned landscaping skills by attending the weekend classes at your nursery and at others. Although I have enjoyed my own business, I look forward to using my skills in a position at your company. In addition, I bring enthusiasm, energy, and a sincere interest in enhancing the value of homes with beautiful landscaping.

I have enclosed my résumé. You can reach me after 3:00 PM any day at 925-4765. Thank you for your consideration.

Sincerely,

Claire Perez

The cover letter introduces you to the employer and highlights your relevant experience.

job. The employer should be able to get a sense of your personality.

If you have not learned how to format a business letter, look at a sample from the Internet or a library. Your name and complete contact information should appear at the top of the letter. Below that is the hiring manager or your contact's name and address. If you don't know all the information, you will need to call to find out the name of the person or address or look it up on the Internet. The salutation comes next. If the hiring manager's name is Mr. Bill Jones, the salutation is "Dear Mr. Jones." Don't forget to use a colon instead of a comma.

Your school or public library will have models of résumés and cover letters that you can look at as you compose yours.

The body paragraphs should explain why you want the job and how your experience and interests fit the position and the company. Make clear what you have to offer to the employer. Conclude your letter with a request to contact the employer at a later date. Finally, do a complete proofread. Just to make sure, have a trusted writer or others proof it as well. Jobs have been lost because of a typo or the use of a homonym instead of the correct word.

Applications, résumés, and cover letters are a reflection of you as a worker. An employer knows that when these documents are done carefully, he or she can assume that the job applicant also will be focused on the job.

Chapter 4

MAKING A GREAT INTERVIEW IMPRESSION

You have networked like crazy. You have filled out what feels like hundreds of applications. Finally, it pays off. You are invited to an interview. How do you nail the job? The first step is to prepare yourself adequately before the interview. The next step is all about being at your best during the interview. Moreover, what you do after the interview can make all the difference in getting the job.

PREPARING FOR THE INTERVIEW

When you step into the interviewer's office, you'll want to be professional and confident. To display this self-confidence and sense of responsibility, you should take the following steps. First, conduct some research to determine exactly what the business or organization does. Maybe it has a website you could read. It will be helpful to go to the work site to find out how long it takes to get there. You do not want to be late for your interview. You can also see how the company's employees dress. This observation will give you a clue about how you should dress for the interview. You may even be able to talk to some employees about their experiences on the job.

Making a good first impression is crucial. The interviewer will make an instant judgment about you based on how you are dressed and how you act. You will want to make sure that his or her judgment is positive. That good impression starts with your choice of clothing. It is possible to dress stylishly and professionally at the same time.

First, make sure your outfit is clean and pressed. A collared, button-down shirt and dress slacks are always appropriate. Girls, if wearing a skirt, understand that your idea of a proper length may be different from your interviewer's. Use your mom's judgment rather than that of a fashion magazine. Make sure your hair is

Employers will be impressed with job applicants who dress and act professionally during the interview.

clean and styled. Wear nice, closed-toe shoes, cover tattoos, and remove all piercings other than one or two in your ears. Although having a breath mint in your mouth is a good idea, chewing gum is not. Nor is wearing heavy makeup, cologne or aftershave, or lots of jewelry. Do not bring a backpack. Carry your résumé in a clean folder or large envelope.

DURING THE INTERVIEW

There are many things you can do to create a favorable impression at the beginning of an interview. Start with getting there fifteen minutes early. Greet receptionists with courtesy. Introduce yourself to everyone you meet with a firm handshake, eye contact, and a smile. Your body language can convey more information to the interviewer than merely your words.

It is smart to have prepared answers to typical interview questions. That way, you can speak without a lot of fillers such as "like" or "um." Here are some examples of questions you may be asked:

- Tell me about yourself.
- Why do you want to work here?
- What distinguishes you from the other applicants?
- What are your strengths and weaknesses?
- What are your goals?

Keep your answers centered on the job. The employer doesn't want to know every place you've lived and gone to school. He or she is trying to find out if you are a good fit for the job. Use your answers to showcase your best qualities. Employers expect to teach you the hard skills of the particular job, such as supervising young

The key to appearing confident during a job interview is to prepare as much as you can ahead of time.

children or stocking the merchandise. What they want to know is if you have the soft skills. Can you show that you are reliable and work well with a team? Do you communicate well and have a strong work ethic? Find examples from school, sports, and extra-curricular activities that prove that you have these qualities.

You should also be ready with questions for your interviewer. Set aside questions about pay and days off until you have been offered the job. Instead, use your questions to show interest in the business or organization. Ask what qualities he or she thinks an employee needs to possess to be successful. What is a typical day like on the job? What are the opportunities to advance? These questions will give you an idea if the job is right for you.

Thank the interviewer at the end of the interview. Ask for a business card. Give the person another firm handshake. Ask when you can expect to hear from him or her about the hiring decision. Keep smiling, and show energy and enthusiasm for the job.

Writing an accurate, courteous thank-you note to your interviewers will leave a lasting, positive impression on them.

FOLLOWING UP AFTER THE INTERVIEW

The interviewer might tell you he or she will call you later. It is essential to follow up with a thank-you note. Even if you have decided that you don't want the job, there may be another job there in the future that you will want. The note should be neatly handwritten with everyone's name spelled correctly. Job search specialist Kelly Sanchez stresses the importance of accuracy. "The system is now designed to weed people out," she told *Marketplace Money* in 2013. "There's so many people looking for work. So the minute that there's a spelling error,

THANK-YOU NOTES

A well-written thank-you note is a good way to demonstrate your communication skills. Using a formal style in the note will showcase your professionalism. One example is the following:

May 28, 2013

Janice Jobless
555 Five Street
Washington, D.C. 20003
(212) 444-4444

Robert Jones
Manager, Food Sales
National Zoo
Washington, D.C. 20004

Dear Mr. Jones:

Thank you so much for interviewing me for the position in the National Zoo snack bar. Being there, meeting you, and hearing your description of the job have made me even more eager for the position. I am certain that my two years of experience in the busy snack bar at my school's sporting events has made me a perfect candidate for the job. My energy and enthusiasm for the position will be a definite plus for your company.

I will contact you next week to see if you have made a decision about the job. I can be reached at (212) 444-4444 after 3:00 PM.

Sincerely,

Janice Jobless

they're not prepared, they show up late, they're calling the business asking for directions—those sorts of things, you're done. They have to have all of their T's crossed and their I's dotted and to stand out."

If the job decision will be made within a day or two, it is acceptable to e-mail the thank-you note. However, make sure to use professional e-mail etiquette. When e-mailing, teens sometimes use the same abbreviations as they do when texting. Put complete information in the subject line, such as "Thank you for the interview for the lifeguard job on May 18." Use your best writing skills, and end with your complete name and contact information.

Whether written or e-mailed, the thank-you note is your last chance to convince the interviewer that you are right for the job. Summarize your qualifications. Express interest and enthusiasm. Mention that you will be following up with a phone call in a week. Record in your job search tracking form the dates of your interview and when you sent the thank-you note. Then keep looking for jobs. The most successful job hunters are the most persistent ones.

Chapter 5

SUCCEEDING ON THE JOB

Congratulations! You've been offered a job! Now you can relax, right? Of course not. There are many things to think about before you accept the job offer. Work hours, transportation, and work attire are all concerns. Once you start the job, you'll need to become a valuable part of the team. Even though you are still a teen, you want to act and be treated like an adult. Your attitude and behavior will determine your success. Following these steps can help you succeed on the job.

CONSIDERING THE JOB OFFER

Take some time to look at all aspects of the job before you accept the offer. The first question you might have could be about the work hours. Remember that school is your top priority right now. Working more than twenty hours each week will negatively affect your progress at school. If the business has early or late hours, find out if you will be expected to open or close. Teens who work late hours will not be able to focus on their coursework during school hours. You can check the U.S. Department of Labor's website Youth Rules! (http://www.youthrules.dol.gov) for labor

Uniforms, work hours, and rate of pay are all important considerations when you are offered a job.

regulations regarding the hours you are able to work legally. Talk to your potential boss about your needs.

Pay and transportation are other concerns to go over when you are offered a job. You may not be able to negotiate your rate of pay. It may be close to minimum wage. Despite that, do politely ask about regular raises. You'll need to understand that raises are tied to your performance on the job. Employees who have the right attitude and behaviors will be rewarded over those who don't. If you do not drive or have a car, figure out your transportation plan. Relying on rides from family members may sometimes put you in a bind. Using public transportation shows your independence and may prove to be more reliable in getting you to work on time.

Before you begin your job, you may have to buy some supplies. Ask how to acquire a uniform if one is expected. You may also need to buy the right type of shoes—for example, nursing shoes, safety boots, or slip-resistant shoes. If there is no uniform required, ask about the dress code. For instance, some businesses may require black or khaki-colored pants worn with the businesses' logo shirt. Many employers are very strict about what you wear, as you represent them to the public. Pay attention to your supervisors' clothing. That attire is a good clue as to how you should dress. Finally, invest in a reliable watch. You'll never want to be late getting back from lunch or a break.

GETTING OFF TO A GREAT START

How can you make a positive impression when you start your job, especially when you are excited and overwhelmed? Despite your feeling nervous, the key is to project an attitude that is friendly, confident, and professional. Your cell phone should be off or on vibrate and stowed in the designated place for your belongings. Try as much as you can to keep smiling because this expression shows friendliness. Introduce yourself to your coworkers and shake

MONEY MATTERS

Successful teens do not spend their hard-earned money as fast as they make it. Instead, they delay gratification and save for the things that they really need. These items could include cell phone bills, car insurance, and college tuition. Setting up savings and checking accounts is a critical step in meeting financial goals. Most businesses can arrange to have your paycheck directly deposited into a bank. If you are under the age of eighteen, you will need a parent or guardian to co-sign your accounts. You will likely get an automated teller machine (ATM) card. Leaving this card at home can help you avoid spending money that you hoped to save.

their hands. Repeating their name after they have given it will help you remember them.

Some teens are shy about asking questions. They think it makes them look dumb. This notion that you look foolish when asking questions is definitely not the case. Your supervisor will be impressed with your interest in the job. Determine exactly what you are expected to accomplish each day.

Be friendly to your coworkers without being excessively social on the job. Show maturity and avoid the workplace drama that can sometimes distract everyone from doing their jobs. Gossip can be toxic in the workplace. Employees who form cliques and exclude others will not be popular. Strive to be a team player.

You also want to be dependable. Nevertheless, you may have to miss a shift at some point. Maybe you are ill or there may be a family commitment you'll need to keep. Give your supervisor notice about having to be out as far ahead as possible. Find someone to take on your responsibilities, if practical. Make sure you call your supervisor yourself about the missed day, instead of a family member. Briefly tell him or her your circumstances and give an idea about when you will return. Take the same kind of action if you will be late to work. Employers will usually be understanding about an occasional late arrival or sick day. Still, employees who have chronic problems will lose their jobs.

GROWING ON THE JOB

Successful professionals are always thinking about how they can grow on the job. They also know that the business succeeds when everyone works together to achieve the same goals. Look for opportunities to be a supportive member of the team. You'll want to be the one who is rewarded with additional responsibilities and higher pay. How can you achieve these rewards? There are some helpful steps to take, including the following.

Go the extra mile. Offer to help your coworkers. Find things to do during downtime. Be assured that your willingness to work hard will be noticed and rewarded. Darmesh Shah, founder of the employment website HubSpot, recommends that new employees "spot the high performers and mimic them." Watch how the best workers make decisions and solve problems. He also suggests that new workers find a way to stand out. Maybe you are the first one to volunteer for a project, or you are always willing to help someone who is struggling. These behaviors will show your employer that you are ready to lead others.

If possible, try to be innovative. You may have to follow strict guidelines. However, look for opportunities to improve procedures or make the business stand out. For example, a young worker at a business in Oregon suggested an idea to her employer. She couldn't find her company on YouTube, but she did find its competition there. "It never occurred to us to even think about being on YouTube," the company president told *IndustryWeek*. In San Diego, California, Beth Henneberg went from unpaid intern to paid employee because of her good ideas. Working for an organization that imported baskets made by women in poverty in Rwanda, Africa, she thought of selling them at local farmers' markets. "They loved that I brought something new to the job," she said.

There is more to a job than learning the particular skills and procedures. The key to success is managing the soft skills. Getting along with coworkers, staying enthusiastic and motivated, and looking for creative solutions to problems are crucial for success. Another important factor is learning on the job and building your career skills. How can you acquire this knowledge and gain these abilities? Many teens may want to look for opportunities in postsecondary education.

Being able to work productively on a team is a critical workplace skill.

Chapter 6

PLANNING FOR CAREER AND POSTSECONDARY OPTIONS

Few people choose a career based on their first job. Yet the jobs you have as a teen can provide valuable clues to choosing a career. For example, you may have enjoyed teaching swimming to children. That teaching experience may lead you to consider a career in education. In the same way, a job in retail might have sparked an interest in business. Working in the fast-food industry might provide insight into your ability to handle fast-paced situations. Regardless of where you worked, you can use your experiences to help you plan for your future. What should you be thinking about as you move through your high school years?

TAKE A RIGOROUS COURSE LOAD IN HIGH SCHOOL

For most people, high school provides a foundation for the rest of their lives. Many students, however, do not take advantage of the opportunities that are available there. You would be smart to take the most challenging courses that you are capable of handling. Honors and Advanced Placement classes will build communication, problem-solving, and study skills. You will develop the discipline and good study habits that will help you learn far into your future.

You might also consider schools and programs that offer vocational and technical education. These might be schools-within-a-school or magnet schools that specialize in one field. For example, Washoe County School District in Nevada offers "Signature Academies." These academies are in such fields as health sciences, digital technologies, sustainable resources, and performing arts. There are encouraging reasons to think about attending a career school or program. According to a 2012 study on teen career readiness, teens who attend career exploration programs have better grades than those who do not. They also have lower dropout rates and do better in college than other students. In some programs, students can earn college credit while they are still attending high school.

GAIN EXPERIENCE WITH JOB SHADOWS AND INTERNSHIPS

Seeing a career up close can give you valuable information for choosing your own. Your school's guidance department or career center may be able to provide a job shadow. A job shadow is an opportunity for you to follow someone in an area of your interest for a day. You can interview various workers about their jobs.

Some schools offer internships. These may last from a few weeks to a semester. Interns get experience in a field while gaining valuable skills, such as efficient time management and effective communication. For example, the National Aeronautics and Space Administration (NASA) offers paid summer internships for high school students with high grade point averages. Students learn about space, robotics, and other science and engineering fields. You

Summer interns work in robotics at NASA's Goddard Space Flight Center in Greenbelt, Maryland. Internships can provide experiences that inspire young people and help prepare them for a career.

may be able to find internships in hospitals, business offices, airports, and zoos. These experiences will impress future employers and colleges.

TIME MANAGEMENT— JUGGLING SCHOOL AND WORK

Teens who work soon discover that time management becomes a huge challenge. It seems as if big demands on the job wait specifically for midterm or finals time at school. Successful time management jugglers rely on an essential tool—a large master calendar. Large wall calendars can help you visualize the big picture and enable you to check your progress frequently. Buy or print from a word processing program a calendar with space to write in each day. Color-code work schedules, school homework, project due dates, and tests. In addition, write in your family events, social obligations, and extra-curricular activities. Calendar applications downloaded to your computer, tablet, iPod, or smartphone are smart ways to stay organized. Most of them can provide reminders of upcoming events. Jam-packed weeks can be red flags that you are taking on too much and that you have too many scheduling conflicts. You may have to set priorities and let some things go.

INVESTIGATE CAREER OPTIONS AFTER GRADUATION

There are many options for high school graduates who aren't interested in going to college or can't afford college tuition. You may be able to prepare for a career by learning on the job or through an apprenticeship. Many hospitals train their own emergency medical technicians (EMTs). Police and fire departments often have their own academies. Preschools, medical

Occupational classes can provide a connection between school and the world of work. In addition, job shadowing can provide the opportunity to learn a job by walking through a day as a shadow to someone who is already working.

offices, and retail businesses are other places where entry-level workers can work their way up to well-paying positions. Your high school preparation may be useful for those occupations

where workers need to pass exams to advance within the organization.

Community colleges and trade schools offer short-term classes in some occupations. For instance, phlebotomists (workers who draw blood), certified nursing assistants, and some computer technicians can start a career with less than one semester of classes. Students interested in the trades such as machinist, electrician, or plumbing can begin apprenticeships. Sales professionals often began with entry-level positions as assistants. Your high school career counselors can steer you in the right direction if you want to pursue one of these career paths.

EARN A COLLEGE DEGREE

Most career experts agree that earning a college degree can greatly boost your earning power. According to a 2012 report from Georgetown University's Center on Education and the Workforce, the unemployment rate for high school graduates is much higher than that for college graduates. Salaries for workers with a bachelor's degree are nearly twice as high as those with only a high school diploma. Students who choose a science, technology,

These people are taking a tour of a college campus. College can be an affordable option for students who are motivated to earn a degree.

engineering, math (STEM) major will fare even better. They can expect higher salaries and lower unemployment rates than many other fields of study.

An associate's degree from a community college is a shorter, lower-cost option for a well-paying career than earning a bachelor's degree. Students can earn their degrees with two years of full-time study. Community college tuition is often half the cost of tuition at universities. Registered nurses, dental hygienists, and computer programmers can find abundant job opportunities in their fields.

Talk to your counselor early in your high school career about your going to college. Attend tours, college fairs, and financial aid information events. Scholarships are available to students who are motivated and study hard. High scores on college entrance exams such as the SAT and ACT can improve your chances for admission and financial aid. It is never too early to begin studying for these tests. Did you know that you can have a test question sent daily to your cell phone?

The high school years can be exciting times for teens who are ready to join the adult world. Getting and keeping a job are big steps toward proving your maturity and independence. Successful workers in any position learn the essential skills of taking responsibility, working as a team, setting goals, and maintaining a positive attitude. These are skills that will carry you from that first job to obtaining further education and your career. Whatever you dream for your future, you can have confidence that you will achieve your goals. Why? You have learned that anything is achievable if you can break it down into smaller steps that move you closer to your dreams.

GLOSSARY

apprenticeship Working for a skilled or qualified person for a specific time in order to learn a trade.

attire Clothing for a specific occasion.

categorize To classify items by their specific qualities.

chronic Continuing for a long time or occurring frequently.

collaboration Working with others to achieve the same goal.

concentric Different-sized circles having the same center.

differentiate To distinguish one thing from another by its qualities.

direct deposit Employers deposit a paycheck into a bank account instead of giving it to an employee.

etiquette Manners, or a code of expected behavior.

gratification Something that gives satisfaction.

hospitality Industry involved with hotels, resorts, and other lodging.

human resources The department of a company that hires employees and maintains their data.

innovative Introducing something new and creative.

internship A formal program that gives practical experience to beginners in an occupation.

mimic To imitate or copy in action.

networking To cultivate people who can be helpful to one professionally.

postsecondary Education or training after high school.

prioritize To arrange in order of importance.

résumé A brief, organized summary of experience and qualifications.

salutation A word or phrase that serves as a greeting in a business letter.

spreadsheet A worksheet, usually arranged in columns, used to make calculations.

systematic Using a specific plan or method.

FOR MORE INFORMATION

American Job Center
U.S. Department of Labor, Employment and Training
    Administration
Francis Perkins Building
200 Constitution Avenue NW
Washington, DC 20210
(877) 872-5627
Website: http://jobcenter.usa.gov
The American Job Center is a one-stop resource for students,
    job seekers, and businesses offering employment and
    training.

College Board
45 Columbus Avenue
New York, NY 10023-6917
(212) 713-8000
Website: http://www.collegeboard.org
The College Board helps students plan, search, apply, and pay
    for college.

Junior Achievement USA (JA)
One Education Way
Colorado Springs, CO 80906
(719) 540-8000
Website: http://ja.org
Junior Achievement is the world's largest organization dedicated
    to educating students about workforce readiness, entrepre-
    neurship, and financial literacy through experiential,
    hands-on programs.

National Youth Employment Coalition (NYEC)
1836 Jefferson Place NW
Washington, DC 20036
(202) 659-1064
Website: http://nyec.org
This organization provides resources for parents, community
members, and youth in career exploration, education,
employment and training, money and finance, and
youth action.

Service Canada
Canada Enquiry Centre
Ottawa ON K1A 0J9
Canada
(800) 622-6232
Website: http://www.servicecanada.gc.ca
This government department provides a wide range of career
services to Canadian citizens.

U.S. Bureau of Labor Statistics (BLS)
U.S. Department of Labor
Postal Square Building
2 Massachusetts Avenue NE
Washington, DC 20212-0001
(202) 691-5200
Website: http://www.bls.gov/home.htm; for *Occupational Outlook
Handbook* Online: http://www.bls.gov/oco
The BLS is the chief fact-finding agency for the federal government
in the area of labor economics and statistics. It describes
numerous jobs and careers, and offers career-related help for
high school students at http://www.bls.gov/k12/index.htm.
It also publishes the *Occupational Outlook Handbook*, which

gives descriptions of more than 250 occupations, required training, working conditions, and pay.

U.S. Department of Labor
Wage and Hour Division
Frances Perkins Building
200 Constitution Avenue NW
Washington, DC 20210
(866) 487-2365
Website: http://www.dol.gov
The U.S. Department of Labor provides information regarding labor laws for young people.

Youth Canada
40 Promenade du Portage, Phase IV, 4D392
Mail Drop 403
Gatineau, QC K1A 0J9
Canada
Attn: Youth Operations Directorate
800-O-CANADA (622-6232)
Website: http://www.youth.gc.ca
This one-stop resource center for Canadian youth contains information on education, employment, health, careers, and finance.

WEBSITES

Due to the changing nature of Internet links, Rosen Publishing has developed an online list of websites related to the subject of this book. This site is updated regularly. Please use this link to access the list:

http://www.rosenlinks.com/WAWR/Hunt

FOR FURTHER READING

Berger, Lauren. *All Work, No Pay: Finding an Internship, Building Your Résumé, Making Connections, and Gaining Job Experience.* New York, NY: Ten Speed Press, 2012.

Fireside, Bryna. *Choices for the High School Graduate: A Survival Guide for the Information Age.* 5th ed. New York, NY: Checkmark Books, 2009.

Gray, Kenneth. *Getting Real: Helping Teens Find Their Future.* Thousand Oaks, CA: Corwin Press, 2009.

Harmon, Daniel E. *First Job Smarts* (Get Smart with Your Money). New York, NY: Rosen Publishing, 2009.

Labovich, Laura M., and Miriam Salpeter. *100 Conversations for Career Success.* New York, NY: Learning Express, 2012.

Lehman, Jeff. *First Job, First Paycheck.* Seattle, WA: Mentor Press, 2011.

Lore, Nicholas. *Now What? The Young Person's Guide to Choosing the Perfect Career.* New York, NY: Simon & Shuster, 2008.

McCormick, Lisa. *Financial Aid Smarts* (Get Smart with Your Money). New York, NY: Rosen Publishing, 2013

Monteverde, Matt. *Frequently Asked Questions About Budgeting and Money Management.* New York, NY: Rosen Publishing, 2009.

Mooney, Carla. *Smart Saving and Financial Planning* (Get Smart with Your Money). New York, NY: Rosen Publishing, 2013.

Morkes, Andrew. *Hot Jobs: More Than 25 Careers with the Highest Pay, Fastest Growth, and Most New Job Openings.* Chicago, IL: College and Career Press, 2010.

Pitts, Pam. *Money 101:14 Things Every Teen Should Know About Money.* Charleston, SC: Butterfly Financial, 2009.

Porterfield, Jason. *Frequently Asked Questions About College and Career Training.* New York: Rosen Publishing, 2008.

Rankin, Kenrya. *Start It Up: The Complete Teen Business Guide to Turning Your Passions into Pay.* San Francisco, CA: Orange Avenue Publishing, 2011.

Reeves, Ellen Gordon. *Can I Wear My Nose Ring to the Interview?* New York, NY: Workman Publishing, 2009.

Scheunemann, Pam. *Cool Jobs for Kids Who Like Kids.* Edina, MN: ABDO Publishing., 2011.

Sember, Brette McWhorter. *The Everything Kids' Money Book: Earn It, Save It, and Watch It Grow!* Avon, MA: F+W Publications, 2008.

Sommer, Carl. *Teen Success in Career and Life Skills.* Houston, TX: Advance Publishing, 2009.

Teen's Guide to College and Career Planning. Lawrenceville, NJ: Peterson's, 2011.

Withers, Jennie, and Denise Dunlap-Taylor. *Hey, Get a Job! A Teen Guide for Getting and Keeping a Job.* Caldwell, ID: Caxton Press, 2009.

BIBLIOGRAPHY

Bissonnette, Barbara. *The Complete Guide to Getting a Job for People with Asperger's Syndrome.* Philadelphia, PA: Jessica Kingsley Publishers, 2013.

Bolles, Richard N., and Carol Christen. *What Color Is Your Parachute? for Teens.* Berkeley, CA: Ten Speed Press, 2006.

Boyd, Alesha Williams, and Michelle Gladden. "More Students Turn to Career Academies." *USA Today*, May 27, 2013.

Cable, Josh. "Tools for Tomorrow's Workforce." *IndustryWeek*, February 16, 2011. Retrieved August 20, 2013 (http://www.industryweek.com).

Department of Labor Office of Disability Employment Policy. "Skills to Pay the Bills." Retrieved August 28, 2013 (http://www.dol.gov/odep/topics/youth/softskills/softskills.pdf).

Eikleberry, Carol. *The Career Guide for Creative and Unconventional People.* Berkeley, CA: Ten Speed Press, 2007.

Gardner, Sarah. "Teens Face Stiff Competition in Search for a Summer Job." *Marketplace Money*, June 21, 2013. Retrieved July 20, 2013 (http://www.marketplace.org/topics/life/teens-face-stiff-competition-search-summer-job).

Georgetown Public Policy Institute. "The College Advantage: Weathering the Economic Storm." Center on Education and the Workforce, August 15, 2012. Retrieved July 21, 2013 (http://cew.georgetown.edu/collegeadvantage/).

Graham, Bridget, and Monique Reidy. *Working World 101.* Avon, MA: Adams Media, 2009.

Henneberg, Beth. *Marketing Assistant, All Across Africa.* Interview with the author, September 3, 2013.

Henneberg, Susan. *Internship Smarts*. New York, NY: Rosen Publishing, 2013.

Labovich, Laura M., and Miriam Salpeter. *100 Conversations for Career Success*. New York, NY: Learning Express, 2012.

The Ladders."Keeping an Eye on Recruiter Behavior." 2012. Retrieved August 29, 2013 (http://cdn.theladders.net/static/images/basicSite/pdfs/TheLadders-EyeTracking-StudyC2.pdf).

Mahoney, Sarah. "8 Job Search Tips for Teens." *Family Circle*. Retrieved August 20, 2013 (http://www.familycircle.com/teen/jobs/job-search-tips-for-teens).

Mehrabian, Albert. *Nonverbal Communication*. Piscataway, NJ: Aldine Transaction, 2007.

NASA. "Internships for Students." 2013. Retrieved August 10, 2013 (https://intern.nasa.gov/ossi/web/public/main/index.cfm?solarAction=view&subAction=content&contentCode=HOME_PAGE_INTERNSHIPS).

Rogers, Kate. "Why Teens Can't Get a Job." Fox Business, January 22, 2012. Retrieved August 28, 2013 (http://www.foxbusiness.com/personal-finance/2012/01/19/why-teens-cant-get-job).

Shah, Dharmesh. "10 Ways to Be Sensationally Successful at Your New Job." LinkedIn blog post, April 29, 2013. Retrieved August 29, 2013 (http://www.linkedin.com/today/post/article/20130429132233-658789-10-ways-to-be-sensationally-successful-at-your-new-job).

Sheridan, Tom. "Teen Jobs: It's a Cold Summer for Out-of-Work Teens." *Press-Enterprise*. July 2, 2013. Retrieved on August 30, 2013 (http://www.pe.com/local-news/riverside-county/temecula/temecula-headlines-index/20130702-teen-jobs-its-a-cold-summer-for-out-of-work-teens.ece).

U.S. Department of Labor, Bureau of Labor Statistics. "Youth Employment in Summer 2012," August 20, 2012. Retrieved August 29, 2013 (http://www.bls.gov/opub/ted/2012/ted_20120822.htm).

Washoe County School District. "Signature Academies." 2013. Retrieved September 16, 2013 (http://www.washoe.k12.nv.us/docs/hs_signature_academies/HS_Signature_Academies_Sponsorship_Needs_Sheet.pdf).

White, Martha C. "In the Math of Education, Two Years Sometimes Is Worth More Than Four Years." *Today Money*, December 30, 2010. Retrieved July 10, 2013 (http://www.today.com/money/math-education-two-years-sometimes-worth-more-four-years-1C7775751?franchiseSlug=todaymoneymain).

INDEX

ABOUT THE AUTHOR

As a parent and high school and community college teacher, Susan Henneberg has been immersed in the world of teens and young adults for more than thirty years. During that time she has been delighted and impressed by their zeal for achieving adulthood. Henneberg has assisted hundreds of teens in finding jobs, becoming successful in college, and passionately working toward their dreams. She teaches and writes in Reno, Nevada.

PHOTO CREDITS

Cover Stephen Coburn/Shuttertsock.com; p. 5 Blend Images/ Moxie Productions/Vetta/Getty Images; p. 8 © Jeff Greenberg/ PhotoEdit; p. 10 © iStockphoto.com/leezsnow; pp. 12–13 bikeriderlondon/Shutterstock.com; p. 15 Mila Supinskaya/ Shutterstock.com; p. 19 Antoine Juliette/Oredia/SuperStock; pp. 20–21 Peter Dazeley/Photographer's Choice/Getty Images; p. 23 Andrey Popov/Shutterstock.com; p. 29 Phase4Studios/ Shutterstock.com; p. 31 Creativa/Shutterstock.com; p. 33 Marilyn Angel Wynn/Nativestock/Getty Images; p. 34 Tracey Whiteside/ Shutterstock.com; p. 38 Goodluz/Shutterstock.com; pp. 42–43 kristian sekulic/E+/Getty Images; p. 46 NASA Goddard/Bill Hrybyk; pp. 48–49 Image Source/Digital Vision/Getty Images; p. 50 Joy Brown/Shutterstock.com; cover and interior graphic elements Artens/Shutterstock.com (figures, urban environment), LeksusTuss/Shuttterstock.com (abstract patterns).

Designer: Brian Garvey; Editor: Kathy Kuhtz Campbell; Photo Researcher: Nicole DiMella